The Emotionally Absent Father

A Path to Healing and Growth

By

Adriana Carey

TABLE OF CONTENTS

INTRODUCTION

In the realm of human relationships, few bonds are as pivotal as that between a father and child. Yet, nestled within the intricate tapestry of familial dynamics lies a profound narrative that resonates with the unspoken struggles of many. "The Emotionally Absent Father" delves into the intricate nuances of this often unexplored facet, casting light on the profound impact of paternal absence on the emotional development of a child. With poignant introspection and a delicate exploration of the human psyche, this book examines the complexities of love, loss, and the never-ending search for understanding and connection. Using heartfelt moments and vulnerability as a lens, it endeavors to navigate the intricacies of the human heart, offering a poignant reflection on the transformative power of empathy, forgiveness, and the enduring hope for reconciliation.

CHAPTER 1

Understanding the Impact of Father Absence

Father absence can have profound implications for individuals and society as a whole. Research has linked it to various negative outcomes such as increased likelihood of behavioral issues, lower academic performance, and higher risk of substance abuse. Additionally, it can affect emotional well-being, contributing to higher rates of depression and anxiety. Understanding these impacts is critical for implementing effective interventions and support systems that can help mitigate the consequences of father absence and foster healthier outcomes for affected individuals.

CHAPTER 2

Exploring the Consequences of Emotional Disconnection

Emotional disconnection can have profound consequences on individuals and their relationships such as:

Strained Relationships: People who are emotionally disconnected often struggle to connect with others on an intimate or empathetic level. This can lead to strained relationships with friends, family, or partners.

Mental Health: Emotional disconnection can contribute to feelings of loneliness, anxiety, and depression. It's important for emotional well-being to have a support system and emotional connections with others.

Communication Issues: It can lead to poor communication, as individuals may have difficulty expressing their feelings or understanding the emotions of others.

Physical Health: Emotional disconnection has been linked to physical health problems, such as increased stress and a weakened immune system.

Work and Productivity: In the workplace, emotional disconnection can hinder teamwork and collaboration, impacting job satisfaction and productivity.

Self-Awareness: Emotional disconnection can prevent self-awareness and personal growth, as it may be challenging to confront one's emotions and work through them.

Coping Mechanisms: Some individuals may develop unhealthy coping mechanisms, like substance abuse, to numb emotional pain caused by disconnection.

It's crucial to recognize emotional disconnection and seek help, such as therapy or counseling, to address the underlying issues and work towards healthier emotional connections.

CHAPTER 3

Father figures' roles in child development

Father figures play a significant role in child development. They contribute to a child's emotional, cognitive, and social development in various ways:

Emotional Support: Fathers provide emotional stability and support, which helps children develop a sense of security and self-esteem. Positive interactions with a father figure can foster emotional resilience.

Role Modeling: Fathers serve as role models for their children, demonstrating appropriate behaviors, values, and problem-solving skills. Children often learn how to navigate the world by observing their fathers.

Cognitive Development: Fathers engage in cognitive activities with their children, stimulating intellectual growth. Interactions such as reading, problem-solving, and discussions contribute to a child's cognitive development.

Social Skills: Father figures help children develop social skills and relationships by providing opportunities for social interactions, teaching cooperation, and imparting values related to interpersonal relationships.

Gender Identity: Fathers play a role in helping children develop their gender identity and understand traditional gender roles. They provide a different perspective from mothers, contributing to a more well-rounded view of the world.

Discipline and Boundaries: Fathers often contribute to discipline and setting boundaries, which are essential for a child's moral and ethical development. They can provide structure and consistency in the child's life.

Supportive Co-Parenting: In two-parent households, fathers and mothers can work together to provide a nurturing environment. Positive co-parenting relationships are vital for a child's well-being.

Diverse Perspectives: Father figures can offer unique perspectives and experiences, enriching a child's worldview and helping them develop empathy and open-mindedness.

 It's important to note that the impact of a father figure can vary based on individual circumstances, but their involvement in a

child's life can have a profound and positive effect on their development.

CHAPTER 4

Psychological effects of Emotionally absent father on children and adults.

The psychological effects of an emotionally absent father on children and adults can be profound and long-lasting. Some common effects may include:

Low Self-Esteem: Children who grow up with emotionally absent fathers often struggle with feelings of inadequacy and low self-worth.

Attachment Issues: A lack of emotional connection with a father can lead to difficulties forming secure attachments in relationships, both as children and adults.

Emotional Regulation Problems: Children may have difficulty regulating their emotions, leading to mood swings, anxiety, or depression.

Trust Issues: An absent father can make it challenging to trust others, leading to difficulties in forming healthy relationships.

Behavioral Problems: Children may act out or engage in risky behaviors as a way to cope with the emotional void left by an absent father.

Struggles with Intimacy: Adults who experienced an emotionally absent father may find it challenging to be emotionally intimate in their relationships.

Gender Identity Issues: Absent fathers can impact a child's understanding of gender roles and identity.

Long-Term Mental Health Effects: The effects of an emotionally absent father can persist into adulthood, contributing to conditions like anxiety, depression, and personality disorders.

It's important to note that these effects can vary from person to person, and not everyone who experiences an emotionally absent father will develop these issues. Therapy and support can be helpful in addressing these emotional wounds and working toward healing and personal growth.

CHAPTER 5

Recognizing and healing the wounds of father absence.

Father absence can lead to various emotional and psychological wounds, including feelings of abandonment, low self-esteem, and difficulties forming healthy relationships. Recognizing these wounds involves acknowledging the impact of the absence, understanding how it has shaped your experiences and emotions, and seeking support from trusted individuals or professionals.

Healing these wounds often involves therapy, counseling, or support groups that focus on addressing father absence-related issues. Additionally, building a strong support network, fostering self-awareness, and engaging in self-care activities can also be helpful in the healing process. Understanding that healing takes time and effort is crucial, and being patient with oneself is important.

CHAPTER 6

Strategies for Reconnecting with an absent father

Reconnecting with an absent father can be a complex and emotionally challenging process. Here are some strategies to consider:

Self-reflection: Take time to understand your own feelings and expectations regarding the reconnection. What are your goals, and what do you hope to achieve from this reconnection?

Communication: Initiate contact through a letter, email, or phone call expressing your desire to reconnect. Express your emotions freely and honestly, but do so with respect.

Patience: Recognize that rebuilding a relationship takes time. Your father may have reasons for his absence that you don't fully understand. Allow him to reply at his own pace.

Seek professional guidance: Consider involving a therapist or counselor to help facilitate communication and provide support during the process.

Boundaries: Set clear boundaries to protect yourself emotionally. Be prepared for the possibility that the reconnection might not lead to the desired outcomes.

Family support: Engage with other family members who may have insights or connections that can help in the reconnection.

Forgiveness: Be open to forgiving past actions, but also prioritize your own well-being. Forgiveness doesn't mean you have to forget or ignore any pain.

Mutual interests: Find common interests or activities that can help you bond and create shared experiences.

Open-mindedness: Be prepared for the possibility that the reconnection may not go as planned. Maintain an open mind and be adaptable in your approach.

Self-care: Ensure you're taking care of your emotional and mental well-being throughout the process. Reconnecting with an absent parent can be emotionally taxing, so self-care is crucial.

Remember that every situation is unique, and the success of reconnecting with an absent father can vary. It's important to prioritize your own emotional health and well-being in this process.

CHAPTER 7

Building a Healthy Relationship with an Emotionally Absent father and Overcoming Trauma

Building a Healthy Relationship with an Absent father:

Self-Reflection: Begin by understanding your own emotions, expectations, and goals regarding your absent father. Reflect on what you hope to achieve by reconnecting.

Communication: Initiate contact with your father in a thoughtful and honest manner. Express your desire to rebuild the relationship and be open to his response.

Patience: Reconnecting with an absent father can be a slow process. Be patient and allow him the time he needs to respond and re-engage with you.

Boundaries: Establish clear boundaries to protect yourself emotionally. These boundaries should help you manage your expectations and prevent further emotional harm.

Therapeutic Support: Consider involving a therapist or counselor who can facilitate communication, provide guidance, and offer emotional support during this process.

Empathy: Try to understand your father's perspective and the reasons for his absence. This can help you approach the reconnection with empathy and reduced resentment.

Overcoming Emotional Trauma with an Absent father:

Acceptance of Emotions: Allow yourself to acknowledge and validate your emotions. It's natural to feel anger, sadness, and confusion due to the absence of a father figure.

Seek Help: Seek emotional support and guidance from friends, family, or a therapist. Talking about your feelings can be a crucial step in healing.

Self-Care: Prioritize self-care by engaging in activities that promote your well-being, such as exercise, a healthy diet, and relaxation techniques.

Forgiveness: Consider forgiving your absent father, not necessarily for his benefit but for your own healing. Forgiveness can alleviate the burden of resentment.

Journaling: Writing about your experiences, emotions, and the process of reconnecting can help you process your feelings and track your progress.

Patience and Time: Healing from emotional trauma takes time. Be patient with yourself and

understand that it's a gradual process, marked by ups and downs.

Remember that building a healthy relationship and overcoming emotional trauma related to an absent father can be a challenging journey. Your well-being is the top priority, so focus on what's best for your emotional health throughout this process.

CHAPTER 8

Case Study : Personal story of healing and Growth.

Certainly, I can share a hypothetical personal story as a case study of healing and growth in the context of an emotionally absent father:

Case Study: Sarah's Journey to Healing and Growth. Sarah grew up in a household with an emotionally absent father. Her father was physically present but rarely engaged with her on an emotional level. He seldom expressed affection or interest in her life, leaving Sarah feeling unimportant and invisible.
As a result, Sarah faced emotional challenges throughout her childhood and adolescence. She struggled with self-esteem, seeking validation from others to fill the void left by her father's emotional absence. She often felt isolated and unable to form deep, meaningful relationships.
However, in her early twenties, Sarah recognized the impact of her father's emotional absence on her life. She decided to embark on a journey of healing and personal growth:
Self-awareness: Sarah began by acknowledging her feelings and the impact of her father's emotional absence on her. This self-awareness was the first step in her healing process.
Therapy: Sarah sought the help of a therapist who specialized in family issues and childhood trauma. Through therapy, she explored her past and learned

coping strategies for dealing with the emotional wounds she carried.

Supportive Relationships: Sarah gradually built a network of supportive friends and mentors who provided the emotional connection she lacked at home. These relationships offered her a sense of belonging and emotional security.

Self-Care: She started focusing on self-care, both physically and emotionally. Sarah learned to nurture herself and prioritize her well-being, which helped boost her self-esteem.

Forgiveness: Sarah worked on forgiving her father, not for his sake but for her own healing. This allowed her to let go of the anger and resentment she held toward him.

Setting Boundaries: Sarah established clear boundaries with her father to protect her emotional well-being. She communicated her needs and expectations in their relationship.

Over time, Sarah's healing and growth became evident:

She gained confidence and a strong sense of self-worth.

Her relationships with friends and partners became healthier and more fulfilling.

Sarah pursued her passions and found a fulfilling career.

She became a mother herself, determined to provide her children with the emotional support and love she had missed.

Sarah's journey is a case study of how one can heal and grow despite the challenges posed by an emotionally absent father. It illustrates the power of self-awareness, therapy, and a supportive network in overcoming the scars of a difficult childhood.

CHAPTER 9

The importance of fatherhood in the society

Fatherhood plays a crucial role in society for several reasons. First and foremost, fathers contribute to the emotional and psychological development of their children. Their involvement fosters a sense of security, self-esteem, and overall well-being in their offspring.

Additionally, fathers often provide financial support, ensuring the economic stability of their families. This financial backing can help secure a child's access to education, healthcare, and a comfortable living environment.

Furthermore, fathers serve as positive role models, imparting values, work ethics, and life skills to their children. Their guidance and involvement can reduce the likelihood of antisocial behavior and delinquency.

In a broader context, responsible fatherhood contributes to family stability and reduces the burden on social welfare systems. It also encourages gender equality by challenging traditional gender roles and promoting shared responsibilities in parenting.

In essence, fatherhood is instrumental in shaping the future generation, strengthening families, and building a more balanced and harmonious society.

CHAPTER 10

Embracing Emotional well-being and resilience

Embracing emotional well-being and resilience despite the absence of a father figure can be a complex and challenging journey. Acknowledging the impact of this absence is crucial, as it allows for the exploration of emotions and the development of coping mechanisms. Fostering a supportive network, engaging in self-care practices, and seeking professional guidance can all contribute to building emotional resilience and fostering a sense of stability and self-worth. By recognizing one's own strength and cultivating a positive mindset, it becomes possible to navigate life's hurdles with greater confidence and emotional balance, despite the absence of a father's presence.

CONCLUSION

The absence of a father figure can have profound and lasting effects on a child's emotional well-being and development, impacting their sense of self, relationships, and overall life trajectory. From heightened vulnerability to mental health challenges, the emotional repercussions of an absent father underscore the critical importance of positive paternal involvement in a child's life. Recognizing the far-reaching consequences of this absence is crucial in fostering support systems and interventions that promote emotional resilience and healing for those affected. Through targeted efforts to provide guidance, mentorship, and emotional support, we can strive to mitigate the impact of paternal absence and cultivate a nurturing environment for children to thrive despite these challenges.

Printed in Great Britain
by Amazon

40990771R00020